Early TOY Encyclopedias

STAR WARS

by Carla Mooney

Early Encyclopedias

An Imprint of Abdo Reference

abdobooks.com

abdobooks.com

Published by Abdo Reference, a division of ABDO, PO Box 398166, Minneapolis, Minnesota 55439.

Printed in China.
052025
092025

THIS BOOK CONTAINS RECYCLED MATERIALS

Editor: Laura Stickney
Series Designers: Candice Keimig, Joshua Olson
Production Designer: Pat Maloney

Library of Congress Control Number: 2024949834

Publisher's Cataloging-in-Publication Data

Names: Mooney, Carla, author.
Title: Star Wars / by Carla Mooney
Description: Minneapolis, Minnesota: Abdo Reference, 2026 | Series: Early toy encyclopedias | Includes online resources and index.
Identifiers: ISBN 9781098297589 (lib. bdg.) | ISBN 9798384930105 (ebook)
Subjects: LCSH: Star Wars films--Juvenile literature. | Motion pictures--Juvenile literature. | Television programs--Juvenile literature. | Toys--Juvenile literature. | Collectibles--Juvenile literature. | Reference materials--Juvenile literature. | Encyclopedias and dictionaries--Juvenile literature.
Classification: DDC 791.4375--dc23

CONTENTS

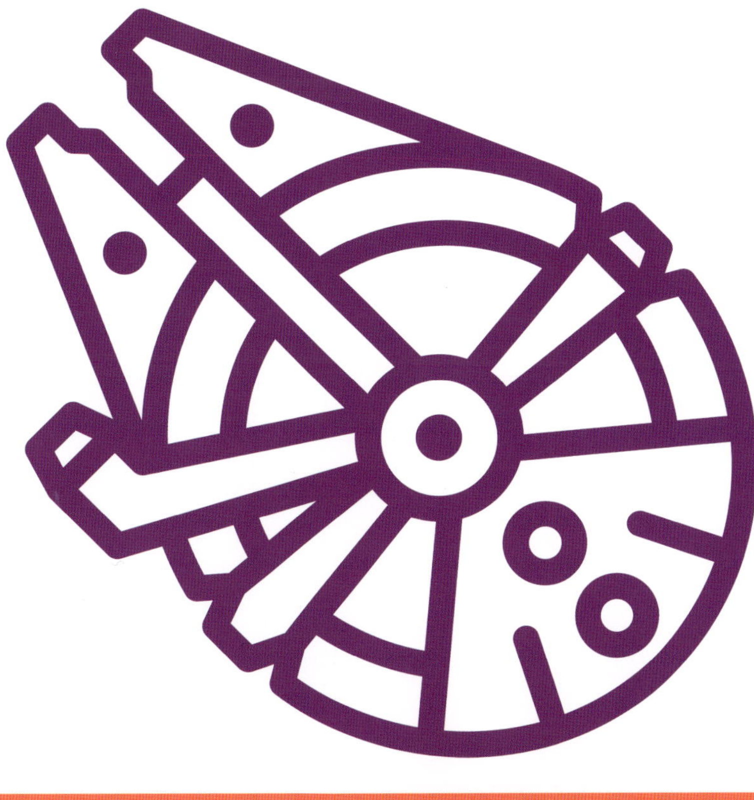

INTRODUCTION

Star Wars Universe

Star Wars has delighted fans for many years. It began as a movie series. The first film was *Star Wars: A New Hope*. It came out in 1977. The movie was a hit. It is set in a galaxy far, far away. It features spaceships and droids. Fans cheered for heroes such as Luke Skywalker and Princess Leia. They fight against Darth Vader and the evil Empire.

Posters for *A New Hope* featured illustrations of major characters in the film. One 1977 poster was designed by British artist Tom Chantrell.

In 1983, hundreds of people lined up outside movie theaters to see the premiere of *Return of the Jedi.* Some fans dressed as their favorite characters.

Pop Culture Sensation

Star Wars took the world by storm. Two sequels soon followed. *The Empire Strikes Back* came out in 1980. *Return of the Jedi* arrived in 1983. Both movies were successful. Star Wars had become a pop culture sensation.

INTRODUCTION

George Lucas started the Lucasfilm production company in 1971. He served as a writer, director, and producer for several Star Wars films.

Finding a Toy Maker

George Lucas created the Star Wars franchise. He wanted to make Star Wars toys. Several companies turned

FUN FACT!

A 1970s oil shortage pushed Kenner to use less oil. Oil is used to make plastic. As a result, the company made its action figures smaller.

him down. But the Kenner company said yes. It took a chance on Star Wars before it was a hit.

Action Figures

Kenner decided to make Star Wars action figures. The company also made playsets and vehicles. The toys let kids recreate scenes from the movies. They could imagine new adventures.

Kenner released its first Star Wars action figures in 1978. It went on to release many popular Star Wars toys throughout the 1970s and 1980s.

Film Franchise Expands

The Star Wars film franchise expanded. Three prequel films were released between 1999 and 2005. These films tell Darth Vader's story. They show how the Empire rose to power. The prequels introduced new characters and worlds.

Sequel Films

Between 2015 and 2019, three Star Wars sequels were released. These movies introduced

The 1999 prequel film *The Phantom Menace* features Anakin Skywalker as a young boy. One toy inspired by the film was an action figure of the character.

new characters. These include Rey, Finn, and Kylo Ren. Original characters also appear. Han Solo is in the films. So are Princess Leia and Luke Skywalker.

More Movies

Several stand-alone Star Wars movies were released. These included *The Clone Wars* (2008), *Rogue One* (2016), and *Solo* (2018). The films tell stories with both new and old characters.

Displays for the first Star Wars sequel, *The Force Awakens*, included pictures of both old and new characters. Harrison Ford and Carrie Fisher returned as Han Solo and Princess Leia in the film.

Star Wars on Television

Star Wars television series have also been popular. One popular show is *The Clone Wars*. This is an animated series. It started in 2008. It tells the story of Jedi Knights. They battle an evil droid army.

The Mandalorian

The Mandalorian is a live-action series. It began in 2019. The show is about a bounty hunter. He travels through the galaxy. The series won several awards. It has also inspired new toys.

There are seven seasons of *Star Wars: The Clone Wars*. The final season came out in 2020.

Star Wars Timeline

Many Star Wars movies and shows take place during different times in the fictional Star Wars universe. This timeline shows the order of various films and shows.

- ***Star Wars Episode I: The Phantom Menace***
- ***Star Wars Episode II: Attack of the Clones***
- ***Star Wars: The Clone Wars***
- ***Star Wars Episode III: Revenge of the Sith***
- ***Solo: A Star Wars Story***
- ***Star Wars Rebels***
- ***Rogue One: A Star Wars Story***
- ***Star Wars Episode IV: A New Hope***
- ***Star Wars Episode V: The Empire Strikes Back***
- ***Star Wars Episode VI: Return of the Jedi***
- ***The Mandalorian***
- ***Star Wars Resistance***
- ***Star Wars Episode VII: The Force Awakens***
- ***Star Wars Episode VIII: The Last Jedi***
- ***Star Wars Episode IX: The Rise of Skywalker***

Expanding Universe

The Star Wars universe has expanded into many areas. These include books, comics, and video games. They all feature Star Wars characters and plots.

Disney's Galaxy's Edge is inspired by planets from the Star Wars films. Visitors can see a full-size replica of the *Millennium Falcon* there.

Today, fans can buy all kinds of Star Wars toys, including character costumes and remote-controlled droids.

Generations of Fans

Since 1977, Star Wars has inspired generations of fans. The franchise is still popular today. And kids continue to play with Star Wars toys.

Star Wars at Disney

Star Wars is featured at Disney theme parks. These are in Florida and California. Fans can step into the Star Wars universe in an area called Star Wars: Galaxy's Edge.

Star Wars: A New Hope **starred Mark Hamill as Luke Skywalker, Carrie Fisher as Princess Leia, and Harrison Ford as Han Solo.**

Surprise Hit

Star Wars: A New Hope came out in May 1977. The movie was a surprise hit. It inspired toys such as action figures. But making these toys would take a long time. They would not be ready for the holiday season.

Early Bird Certificate

Kenner had an idea. The company sold an Early Bird Certificate Package. This contained stickers and a display stand. It included a fan club card. It also had a coupon inside. Kids could mail the coupon. Months later, they would get the first four action figures in the mail.

Ads for the Early Bird Certificate Package included instructions for purchasing and mailing. Many people purchased the packages during the 1977 holiday season.

Making Action Figures

Kenner took several steps to make an action figure. First, workers made a model. An artist sculpted the model from wax. Then artists used tools to add details.

Most Kenner Star Wars figures were designed to have hands that could hold weapons. The original Luke Skywalker figure held a lightsaber.

Kenner's Star Wars figures had highly detailed sculpts. The C-3PO figure had intricate golden plating, just like the droid in the films.

Sculpting

Some artists used a material called acetate. It was similar to carving a block of clay. Artists sculpted the figure in several pieces.

Making Molds

Next, the finished model was used to make molds. Workers poured silicone over the wax model. It hardened. Then it became a mold.

Hardcopies

The silicone mold was used to make a hardcopy. This is a hard plastic copy of the original

Kenner made multiple molds of some Star Wars figures. The "Big Head" Han Solo was made with a larger head than those on other Han Solo figures.

Kenner made many unique molds and hardcopies to capture the wide variety of characters in the Star Wars films. Some people collect these early models.

figure model. The hardcopy was used to make steel molds. Finally, these molds were used to make the figures.

Pouring Plastic

Workers melted hard plastic. Then they poured it into a steel mold. The plastic cooled and hardened. Then the mold was opened. The plastic piece was removed. Most Star Wars figures were made in pieces. The pieces fit together to make the figure.

Some Kenner Star Wars figures had unique pieces. The 1977 R2-D2 figure had a rotating dome headpiece.

Finishing Touches

Next, each figure was painted. Some figures were made entirely from plastic. Others had fabric clothing or capes.

Kenner's 1977 Princess Leia figure had a cape made of a material called vinyl. The cape was removable.

Packaging

Most Star Wars action figures were sold individually. The figure was packaged in a plastic bubble. The bubble was attached to a cardboard back.

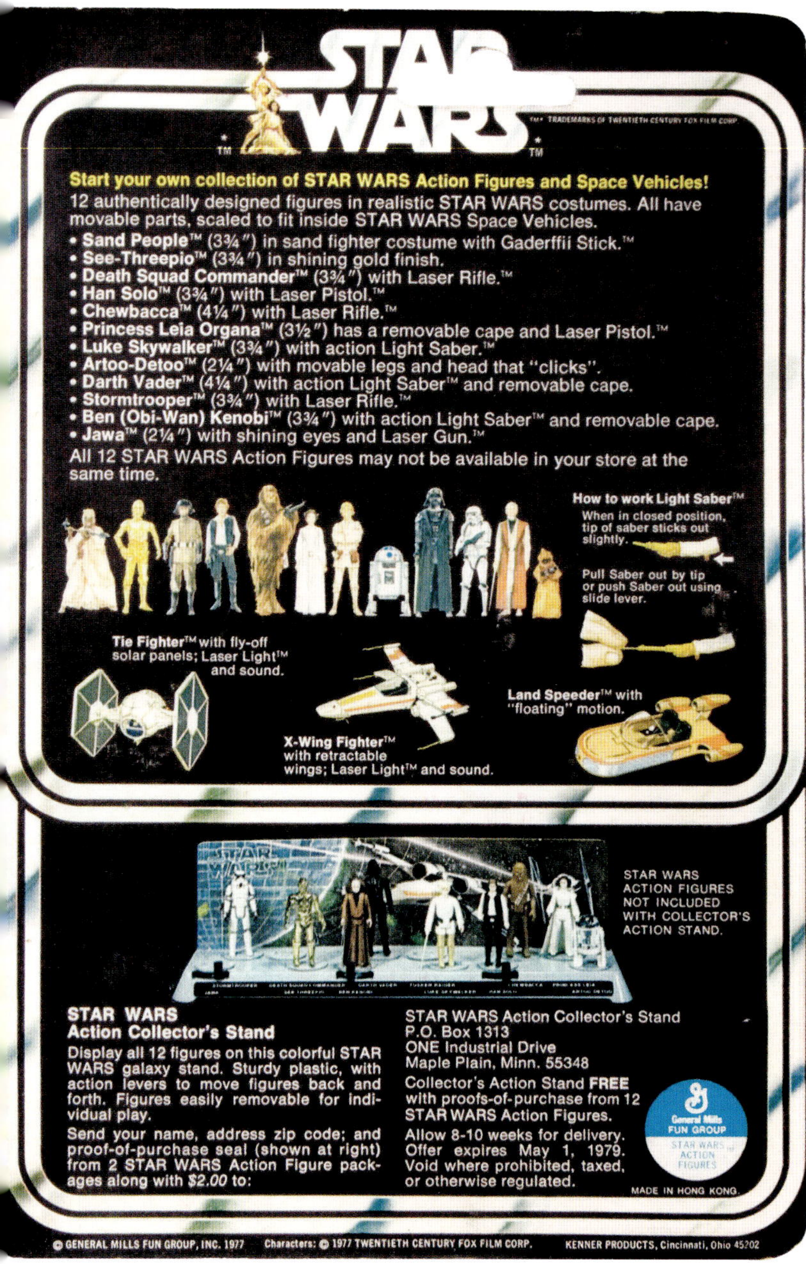

The back of a Kenner Star Wars figure's packaging had instructions and pictures. The first 12 figures are called "12 backs" since they were shown on the packaging.

First Wave

The first wave of Star Wars action figures arrived in 1978. It included 12 figures. Chewbacca, Princess Leia, R2-D2, and Luke Skywalker were the first ones available. They were in the Early Bird package.

Kenner's Early Bird figures came with plastic pegs. These allowed kids to attach the figures to the cardboard stand included in the Early Bird Certificate Package.

Five Moving Parts

Early Bird figures were 3.75 inches (9.5 cm) tall. They had five moving parts. These were their arms, legs, and heads.

Kids could put Kenner Star Wars figures into basic poses. They could raise the figures' arms or turn their heads to the side.

Main Characters

Kenner made its figures look like the movie characters. The R2-D2 figure had

Collectible Toys

Many people collect Star Wars action figures. The most valuable figures are unopened in the original packaging.

movable legs. It had a dome head. The head turned and clicked. Chewbacca carried a special gun. Princess Leia was dressed in white. She wore a cape. Luke Skywalker had a yellow lightsaber.

Unlike the other Early Bird figures, the Chewbacca figure did not have a turning head.

Darth Vader

Darth Vader was one of the most popular Kenner figures. The villain wore a black cloak. He carried a red lightsaber.

The original Darth Vader figure came with an extendable lightsaber. A thin piece could slide out of the lightsaber blade, making it longer.

Other Villains

Figures of other Star Wars villains were created too. Stormtroopers carried out Darth Vader's orders. The Death Squad Commander worked on the Death Star. This is a space station. The figure wore a gray uniform and black helmet. He had a blaster gun.

FUN FACT!

Some early Star Wars figures had a lightsaber built into their arms. The lightsabers could extend out of the arms.

The Death Squad Commander figure was later renamed Star Destroyer Commander.

Fan Favorites

The first wave of action figures included Obi-Wan Kenobi. He wore a vinyl cape. He carried a blue lightsaber. Another figure was Han Solo. This hero had a blaster gun. There was also a C-3PO figure. He looked just like the film's golden droid.

Some early Obi-Wan Kenobi figures had white hair, while others had gray hair.

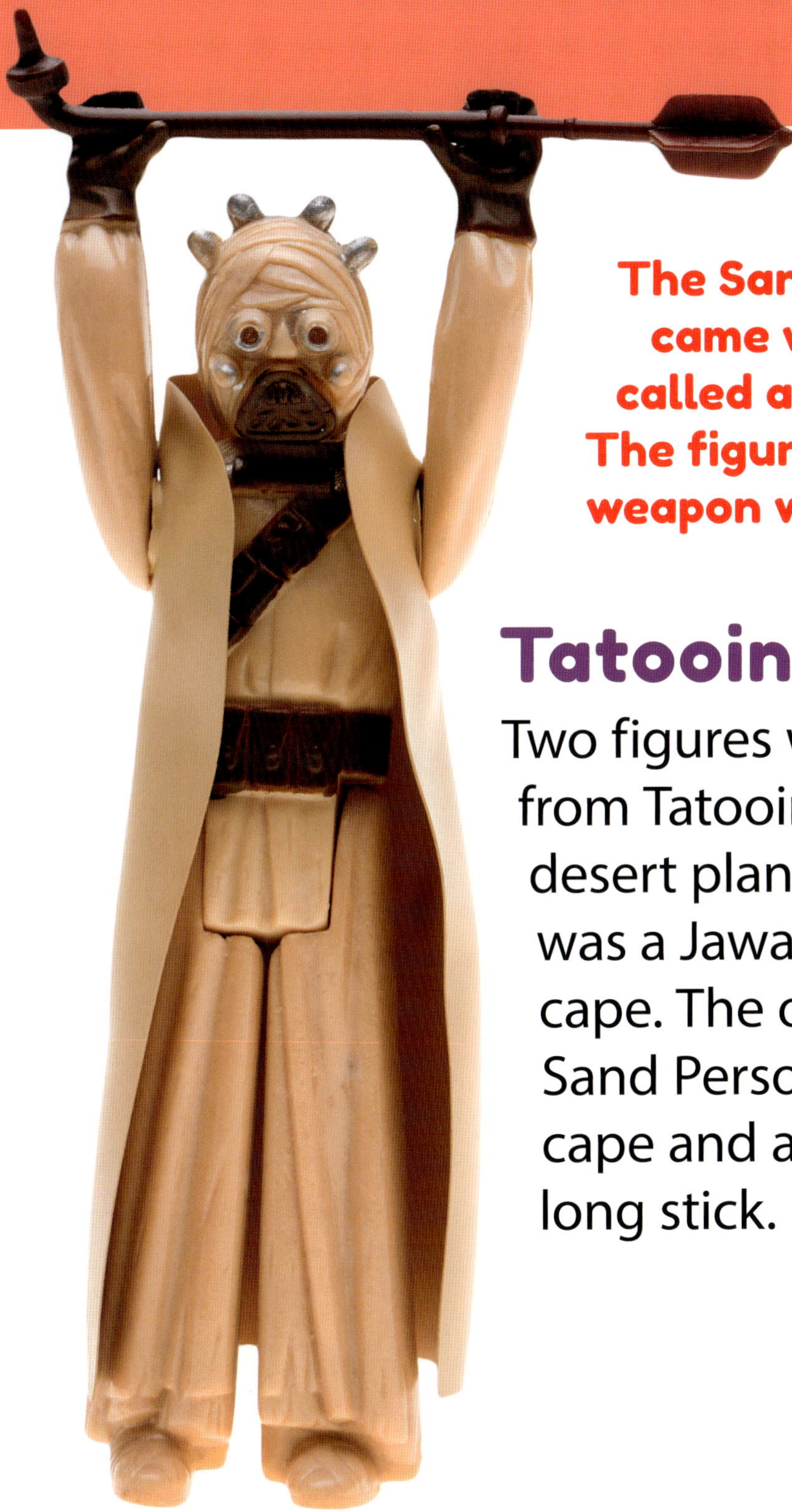

The Sand Person figure came with a weapon called a Gaderffii stick. The figure could hold the weapon with both hands.

Tatooine Figures

Two figures were characters from Tatooine. This is a desert planet. One figure was a Jawa. It wore a brown cape. The other was a Sand Person. It had a beige cape and a long stick.

FUN FACT!

The first Star Wars action figures sold for $1.49 each in 1978.

Greedo appeared in a famous scene with Han Solo in *A New Hope*. Kenner's Greedo figure was bright green and carried a blaster.

Second Wave

Kenner released a second wave of action figures. It came out in 1978 and 1979. It included eight new figures. Some were from Tatooine's Cantina bar. These included Greedo and Hammerhead. They are aliens. Other figures were Snaggletooth and Walrus Man.

Droids

The second wave included three new droid figures. These included the Death Star Droid and Power Droid. Another figure was an R5-D4 droid. Droids have many roles in the Star Wars universe.

The R5-D4 figure had red details and a head that clicked when it turned.

12-Inch Figures

Kenner released a series of 12-inch (30.5 cm) Star Wars figures from 1978 to 1980. The line did not meet expectations. It was discontinued.

X-Wing Luke

Kenner also made new figures of main characters. These figures wore different outfits. Luke Skywalker was the first to get a new outfit. It was the Luke Skywalker X-Wing Pilot figure.

The Luke Skywalker X-Wing Pilot figure wore a bright orange pilot uniform. His round helmet had a Rebel Alliance symbol printed on it.

Boba Fett

Boba Fett is a bounty hunter. Kenner offered the first Boba Fett figure as a mail-in order. Later, a figure was sold in stores.

FUN FACT!

Kenner sold 80 million Star Wars toys in the two years after *Star Wars: A New Hope* came out.

One early version of the Boba Fett figure came with a missile-shooting feature. This toy is rare and has sold for thousands of dollars at auctions.

The Empire Strikes Back featured new Star Wars planets and creatures. Part of the story involves a romance between Han Solo and Princess Leia.

The Empire Strikes Back

In 1980, *The Empire Strikes Back* arrived in theaters. This movie continues the first film's story. It features the same characters. Luke Skywalker, Princess Leia, and Han Solo appear. They battle

Darth Vader. Fans loved the movie. It was a big hit.

New Figures

Kenner made a new series of Star Wars figures. They came out between 1980 and 1982. There were 29 figures. They were released in three waves. Kids could re-create scenes from the movie with these figures.

A new version of Han Solo was included in the first wave of *The Empire Strikes Back* figures. He came in a blue coat that had a gun holster.

On Hoth, Princess Leia wears a white jumpsuit, a vest, and a braided hairstyle. This outfit was featured in Kenner's second wave of *The Empire Strikes Back* figures.

Old Favorites

Some figures were new versions of characters. *The Empire Strikes Back* begins on Hoth. This is an ice planet. Kenner offered new Han Solo, Princess Leia, and Luke Skywalker figures. They wore Hoth uniforms.

Battle of Hoth

In the movie, Rebel soldiers and Stormtroopers battle on Hoth. Kenner released several figures based on this battle. These included the Rebel Soldier and Rebel Commander. There was an Imperial Stormtrooper figure too. These figures had Hoth battle uniforms and guns.

Kenner's Imperial Stormtrooper figure is also known as the Snowtrooper.

Kenner released a Darth Vader Collector's Case as part of its Empire Strikes Back toy line. Kids could store Star Wars action figures in the case.

Rebels in Cloud City

In the movie, the Rebels visit Cloud City. This is a floating city. It is on the planet Bespin. New figures featured characters wearing Bespin clothing. These included Han Solo, Princess Leia, and Luke Skywalker.

Lando Calrissian

The Empire Strikes Back features Lando Calrissian. He is Cloud City's leader. He is also Han Solo's friend. At first, Calrissian betrays the Rebels. He helps Darth Vader capture them. Later, he joins the Rebels. His action figure had a blue shirt and gray cape. It came with a blaster gun.

Some versions of the Lando Calrissian figure have teeth that are painted white, while others do not.

Yoda

Yoda appears in *The Empire Strikes Back*. He is a powerful Jedi master. Luke Skywalker finds him on the planet Dagobah. Skywalker asks Yoda to train him. The Yoda

Early versions of Kenner's Yoda figure came with either an orange or brown snake. The snake could be draped around the figure's neck.

action figure wore a cloth robe. He carried a snake and staff.

Bounty Hunters

Bounty hunters appear in *The Empire Strikes Back*. Their mission is to find the *Millennium Falcon*. This is Han Solo's ship. The bounty hunters want to capture the ship's crew. Kenner created several bounty hunter figures. These included Bossk and IG-88.

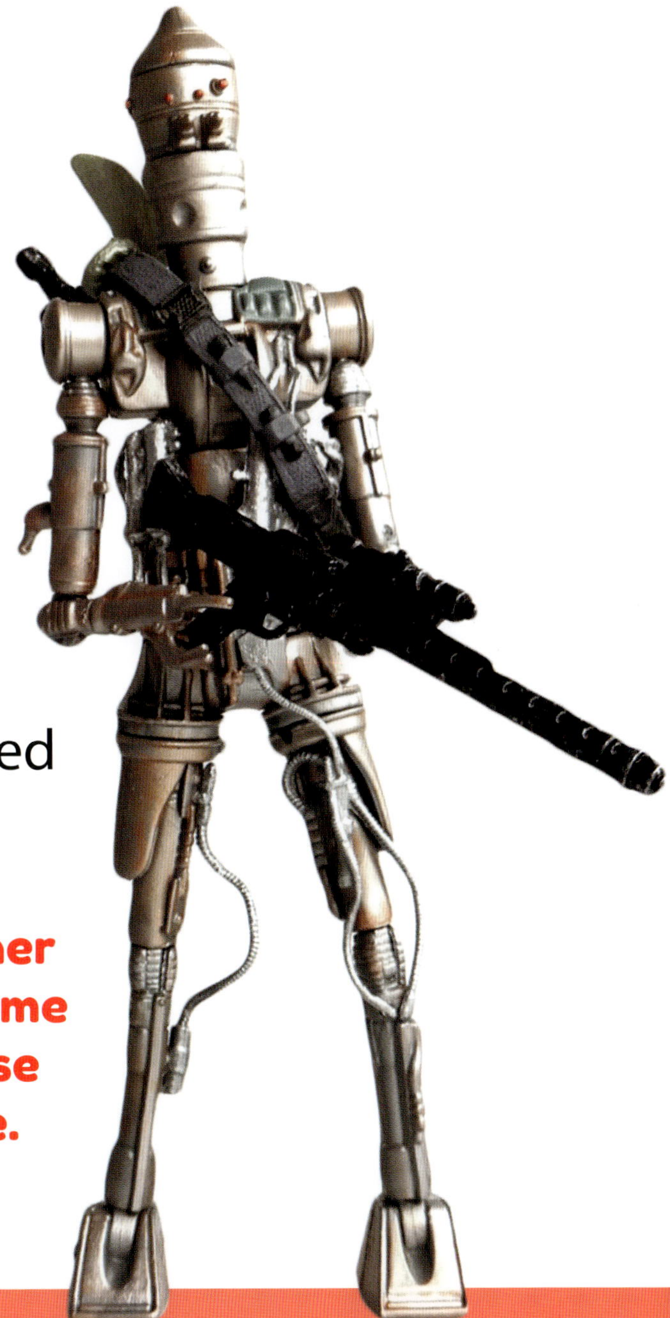

IG-88 was the first Kenner Star Wars figure that came with two weapons. These were a blaster and rifle.

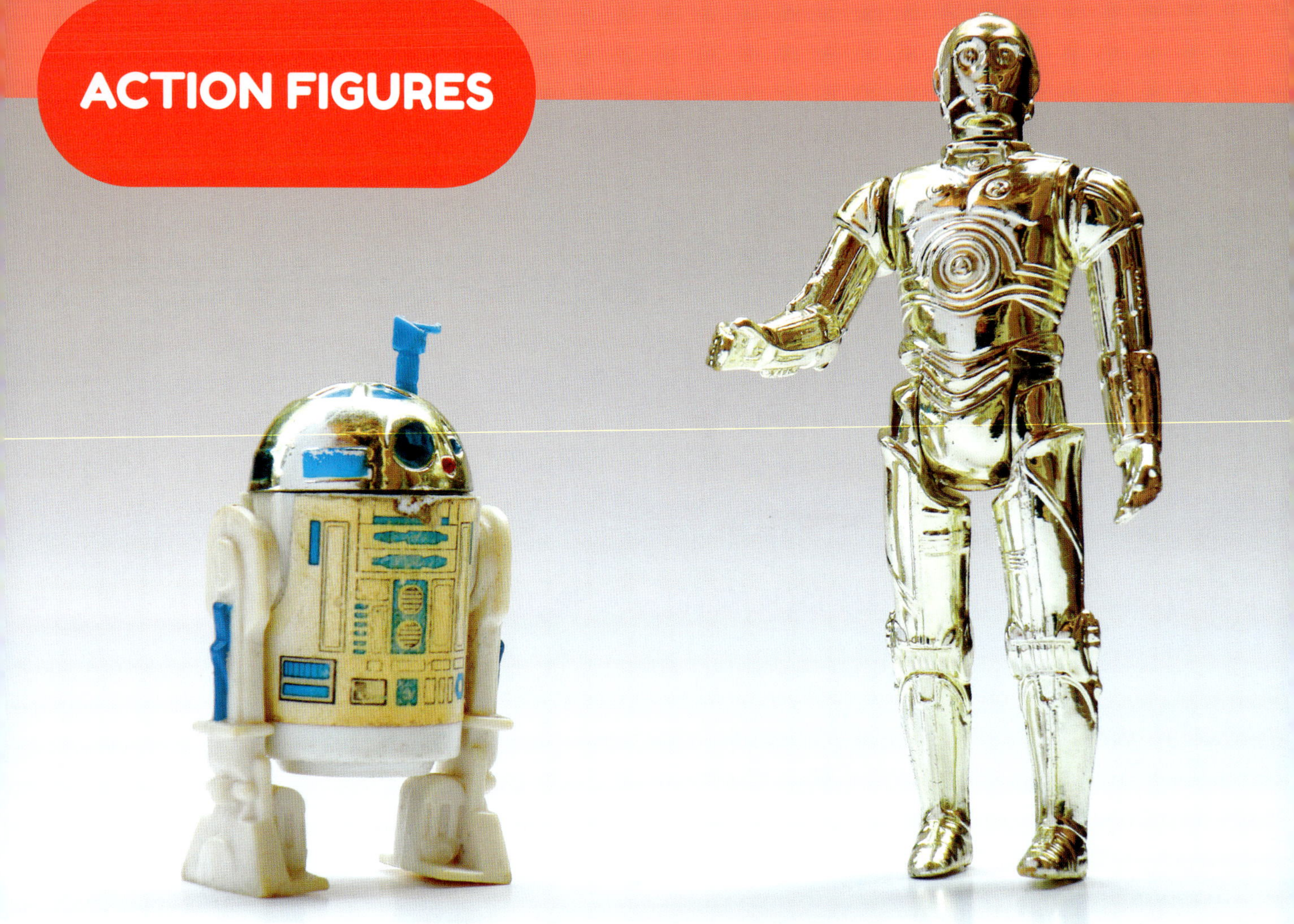

The 1980 R2-D2 figure's sensorscope was bright blue. It extended out of the droid's silver headpiece.

R2-D2 with Sensorscope

In 1980, Kenner released a new R2-D2 figure. It had a sensorscope. This tool could be extended. In the films, R2-D2 uses it to communicate with Luke Skywalker.

New C-3PO

A new C-3PO figure had removable limbs. It came with a backpack. Other figures, such as Chewbacca, could wear the backpack. They could carry C-3PO's limbs in it. This happens in the movie.

The second version of C-3PO had the same shiny gold plating as the original figure. On the packaging, the toy's name sometimes appeared as "See-Threepio."

Return of the Jedi features a dramatic duel between Luke Skywalker and Darth Vader. The battle takes place inside the second Death Star.

Return of the Jedi

The third Star Wars film hit theaters in 1983. It is called *Return of the Jedi*. It features more battles between the Rebels and the Empire. It inspired 31 new action figures. These came out between 1982 and 1984.

Familiar Faces

Kenner produced new versions of Star Wars characters. Luke Skywalker wore a Jedi Knight outfit. Princess Leia had new outfits from *Return of the Jedi*. She wore a combat uniform. She carried a blaster gun. New Han Solo and Lando Calrissian figures were also made.

Micro Collection

Kenner released a Micro Collection of metal playsets. These came out between 1982 and 1983. Each playset came with mini metal figures.

One *Return of the Jedi* Princess Leia figure came with a green combat poncho and a removable helmet.

Ewoks of Endor

Return of the Jedi features Ewoks. They are furry creatures. They live on Endor. They help the Rebels. Kenner made action figures of Ewoks. These included Chief Chirpa, Logray, and Wicket W. Warrick.

In *Return of the Jedi*, Chief Chirpa leads the Ewoks. Kenner's Chief Chirpa figure came with a staff and a removable hood.

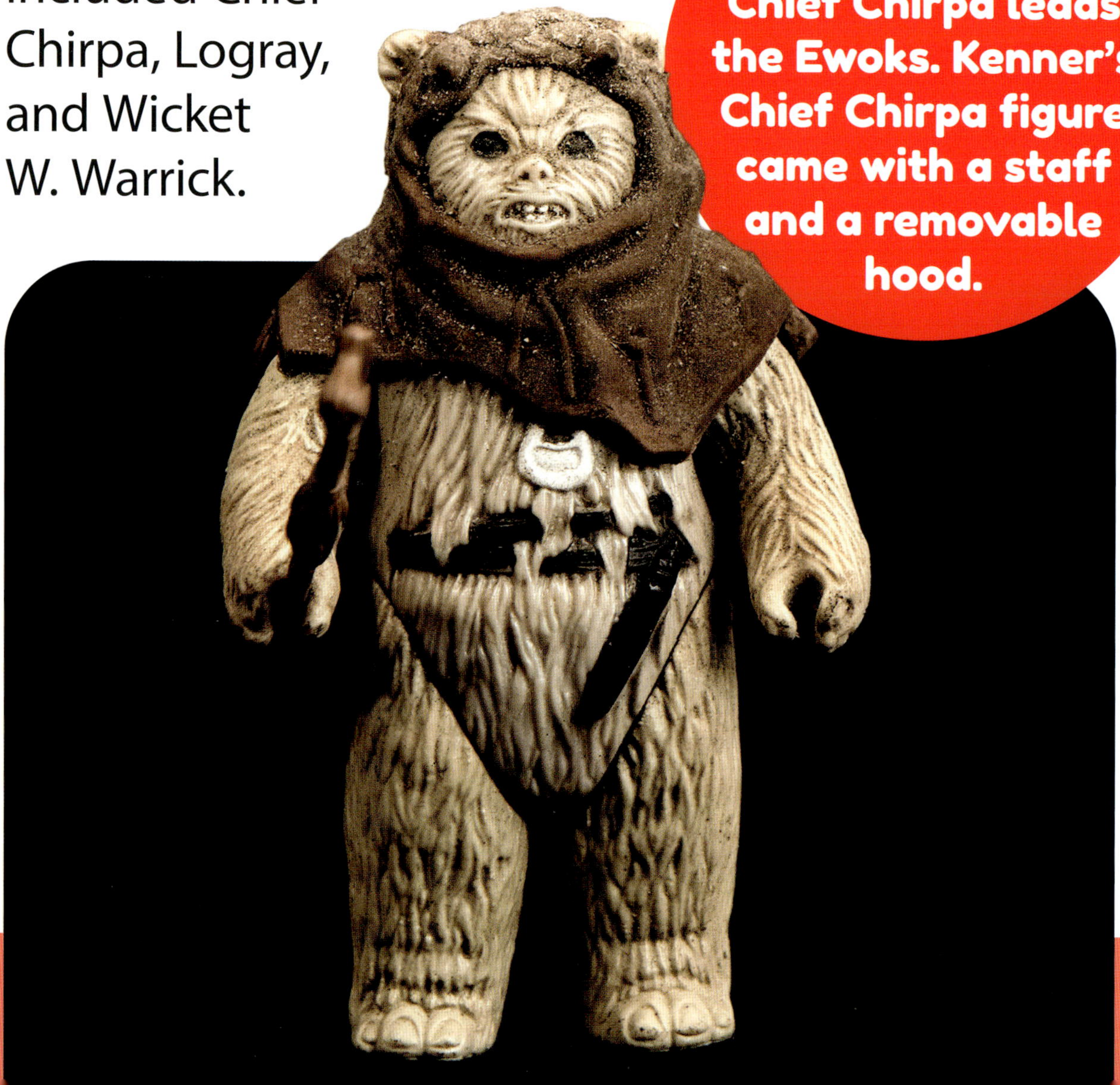

The Emperor

Emperor Palpatine is in *Return of the Jedi*. He is the Empire's leader. He rules over Darth Vader. Palpatine also uses the dark side of the Force. The Force is a kind of energy. It surrounds all living things. Kenner released an Emperor figure in 1984.

The Emperor is also known as Darth Sidious. Kenner's Emperor figure wore a black cloak and had yellow eyes.

After the Trilogy

After 1983, there were no new Star Wars movies for many years. But new toys continued to come out. Kenner released three toy lines in 1985. One was The Power of the Force. It included figures with collector's coins.

Star Wars: Droids

The Droids was another toy line. It was based

The Power of the Force line included a Luke Skywalker figure in an Endor battle outfit. The coin that came with the toy featured a picture of Luke on a speeder bike.

The Droids toy line included a figure of the alien Vlix. Today, this action figure is considered rare.

on *Star Wars: Droids*. This was a television series. The cartoon followed the adventures of R2-D2 and C-3PO. The Droids line included 12 action figures. Each came with a golden collector's coin.

Star Wars: Ewoks

After *Return of the Jedi*, two spin-offs were made for television. They featured Ewoks. Kenner created the Star Wars: Ewoks toy line. It released six Ewok figures. Each included a golden collector's coin.

Hasbro Partnership

After 1985, demand for Star Wars toys slowed. Kenner discontinued its Star Wars action figures. In 1991, toy maker Hasbro bought Kenner. This meant Hasbro could make Star Wars toys.

Hasbro's first Star Wars toy line was known as The Power of the Force 2. It included 26 action figures, including one of Boba Fett.

Renewed Interest

In 1997, the Star Wars trilogy was re-released in theaters. Hasbro made new Star Wars action figures. At first, it made the figures under the Kenner brand. In 1998, Hasbro rebranded the figures. It used its own name.

In 1998, Hasbro released The Power of the Force 2 figures that came with mini movie slides. One was a Darth Vader figure with a removable helmet.

Prequel Trilogy

The long wait for more Star Wars movies ended in 1999. A new prequel trilogy began. These movies take place before the original films. They told new stories. The films introduced new generations to Star Wars. They also renewed interest in Star Wars toys.

Several Padmé Amidala figures were included in Hasbro's Phantom Menace line. One featured the character in a Naboo battle outfit. Her CommTech Chip had four lines.

To use an action figure's CommTech Chip, people had to buy Hasbro's CommTech Reader toy. Touching the chip to the reader activated the sound effects.

The Phantom Menace

The Phantom Menace was released in 1999. Hasbro made 38 new action figures. These figures included a new accessory. It was a CommTech Chip. Each chip played lines from the movie.

Attack of the Clones

The second prequel hit theaters in 2002. It is called *Attack of the Clones*. Hasbro released the Star Wars Saga toy line. It came out between 2002 and 2004. One new figure was Jango Fett. He is a bounty hunter. He is Boba Fett's father.

Revenge of the Sith

The final prequel film was released in 2005.

One Star Wars Saga figure featured Jar Jar Binks in a Gungan senator robe. The toy came with an Electropole weapon.

In *Revenge of the Sith*, General Grievous is known for hunting Jedi Knights and stealing their lightsabers.

It is *Revenge of the Sith*. Hasbro released its Revenge of the Sith toy line in 2005. General Grievous was one new figure. He had four arms. He had four lightsabers.

Cartoon Clones

Hasbro released a line of action figures based on *The Clone Wars* television series. The figures were designed to look like the cartoon's characters. They included Anakin Skywalker, Obi-Wan Kenobi, and Ahsoka Tano. The line lasted from 2008 to 2011.

Change in Focus

In the 2010s, the toy industry changed. Construction toys became more popular. Interest in action figures declined. Oil prices rose. Oil was used to make action figures. This made it more expensive to make detailed Star Wars figures.

Hasbro's Clone Wars line included action figures of clone troopers.

Between 2010 and 2013, Hasbro released the Vintage Collection. This toy line included detailed action figures of many characters, such as Admiral Ackbar.

Two Lines

Since 1978, adults and kids had collected the same Star Wars toys. That changed in 2013. Hasbro split its Star Wars line. One line was for adult collectors. The other line was for kids.

FUN FACT!

Star Wars action figures were inducted into the National Toy Hall of Fame in 2012.

Black Series

Hasbro introduced the Black Series in 2013. This featured 6-inch (15 cm) action figures. Black Series figures were designed for collectors. They were detailed. They had flexible joints. They were also more expensive than other figures.

Hasbro's Black Series action figures are known for having life-like details. Many people collect these figures.

Hasbro's smaller Black Series figures came in black packaging. The line featured many unique Star Wars characters, such as the Jedi Knight Bastila Shan.

For Kids

Hasbro also made 3.75-inch (9.5 cm) Black Series figures. These smaller figures were for kids. To keep costs down, Hasbro made them less detailed. They also had fewer moving parts.

Star Wars: Rebels

Star Wars: Rebels was an animated television series. It ran from 2014 to 2018. Hasbro released 25 figures based on the show. These included Ezra Bridger and Kanan Jarrus.

Sequel Trilogy

A new sequel trilogy began in 2015. The sequels take place after *Return of the Jedi*. The films introduce several new heroes. One is Rey. There are also new villains. These include Kylo Ren.

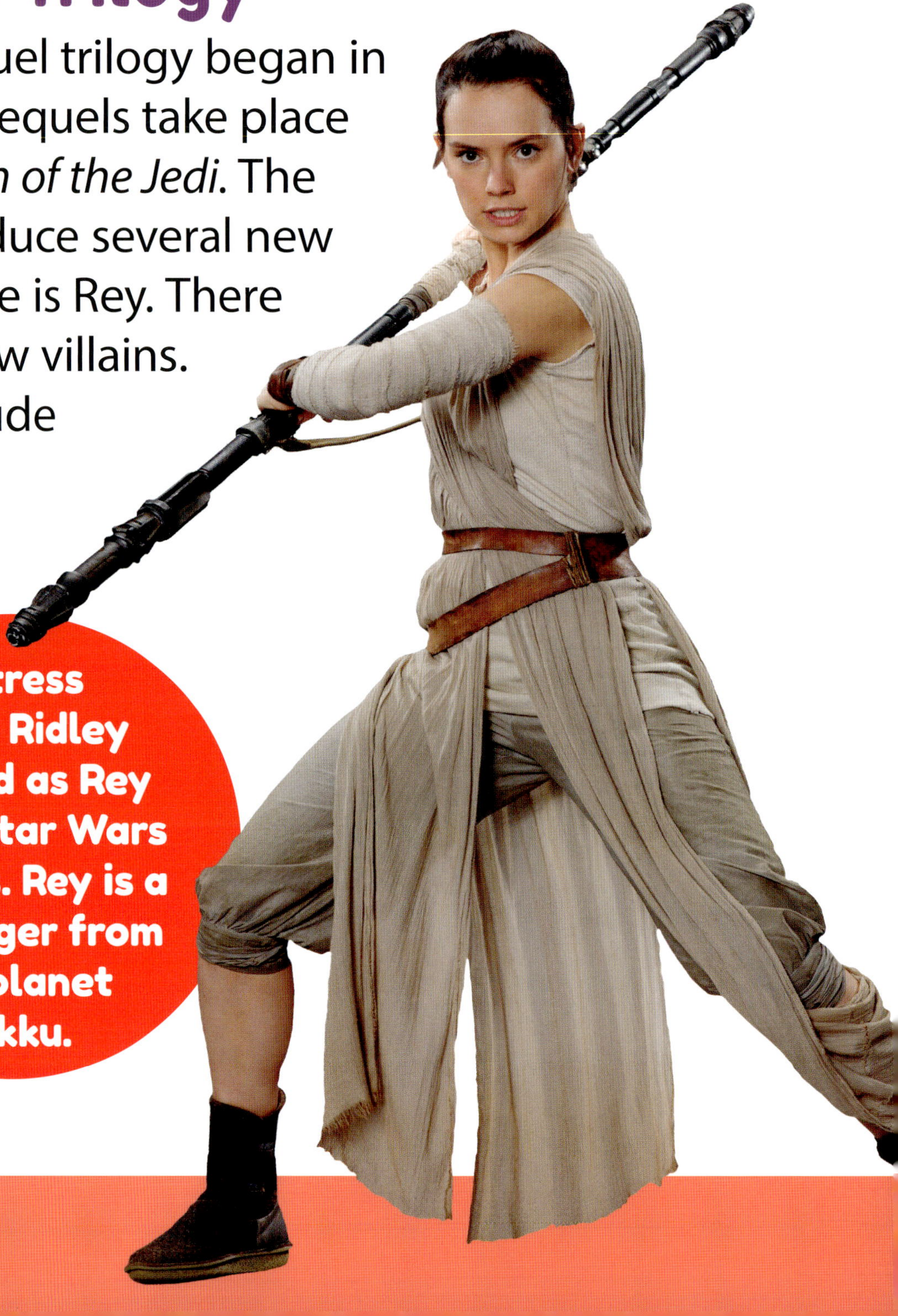

Actress Daisy Ridley starred as Rey in the Star Wars sequels. Rey is a scavenger from the planet Jakku.

The Force Awakens toy line included several Finn figures. One came with a blaster and removable armor.

Marketing Force

New toy lines helped audiences rediscover Star Wars. Hasbro released new action figures. They came out in September 2015. This was three months before the new movie came out. Star Wars fans flooded stores. They wanted to buy the toys.

The Force Awakens

The Force Awakens hit theaters in December 2015. Hasbro released 36 new action figures. They came out in 2015 and 2016. There were figures of Rey, Finn, and Kylo Ren.

In *The Force Awakens*, Kylo Ren wields a unique red lightsaber that has three blades. Hasbro's Kylo Ren action figures came with a miniature version of this weapon.

The Last Jedi

The next movie was *The Last Jedi*. It hit theaters in 2017. Hasbro released 22 action figures that year. Some were new characters such as Rose Tico. Others were fan favorites. These included a new Rey figure. She wore a Jedi training outfit.

Armor Up

A series of Armor Up figures was released for *The Force Awakens*. Each figure had a set of armor. It could be worn or removed.

Mark Hamill returned as Luke Skywalker in *The Last Jedi*. In the film, Luke helps Rey train to be a Jedi.

One Force Link 2.0 set came with action figures of Rey and an Elite Praetorian Guard. The Rey figure had a Jedi training outfit.

Force Link 2.0

The Last Jedi figures had a new feature. It was called Force Link 2.0. Kids could wear a special wristband. They held an action figure near the band. This made the figure play sounds.

The Rise of Skywalker

The Rise of Skywalker arrived in theaters in 2019. Hasbro released the movie's toy line in October 2019. Figures included Kylo Ren, Rey, and a Sith Jet Trooper. These figures were 6 inches (15 cm) tall. Others were 3.75 inches (9.5 cm) tall. One was a blue R2-SHP droid.

***The Rise of Skywalker* features major plot twists and several epic battle scenes.**

More Ways to Play

Kenner created more toys to go with its action figures. They made playsets and creatures. They made accessories. Kids could use the toys and action figures together.

Star Wars Creatures

In 1978, Kenner released its first Star Wars creature. It was the

The 1978 Patrol Dewback toy had movable legs and a head that turned. It came with a harness and saddle.

Patrol Dewback. Action figures could ride on the creature's back. Later, Kenner made Tauntaun and Wampa figures. These creatures are from *The Empire Strikes Back*. Another figure was the Rancor Monster. It is from *Return of the Jedi*.

FUN FACT!

A Tauntaun is a snow lizard that has two sets of nostrils.

In *The Empire Strikes Back*, the Rebels ride Tauntauns while traveling around Hoth. These furry creatures walk on two legs and have curvy horns.

Star Wars Playsets

Playsets expanded how kids could play with action figures. Each playset re-created part of a Star Wars movie. Some playsets had moving parts. Some had an elevator lift. Others had a rope swing.

One 1980 Kenner playset was the Imperial Attack Base. It came with a collapsing snow bridge and a rotating cannon.

Early Playsets

Kenner released its first Star Wars playsets in 1978.

In 1979, Kenner released the Creature Cantina Action playset. It included a cardboard backdrop and a bar.

They featured many settings. These included the Cantina and the Death Star. The Cantina Adventure set was popular. It came with four action figures.

In *The Empire Strikes Back*, Yoda lives on the swampy planet of Dagobah. Luke Skywalker visits the planet to train with Yoda.

Empire Strikes *Back* Playsets

Empire Strikes Back playsets came out in 1980. One popular set was Dagobah Action. It featured Luke Skywalker and Yoda. It included levers. Kids pushed these. This made cargo boxes rise as Luke trained.

Return of the Jedi Playsets

In 1983, Kenner released the Ewok Village playset. It came with accessories. These included a firepit and drum. It also came with a net and a swinging boulder. It even included a throne. C-3PO sits on this in the movie.

The 1983 Ewok Village playset featured a platform built around three large tree trunks. It also included a rope elevator and three huts.

Jabba's Palace

The Jabba the Hutt Action playset was also released in 1983. It came with a large Jabba the Hutt figure. It could sit on a throne. Another playset featured the dungeon at Jabba's palace.

In *Return of the Jedi*, Jabba the Hutt is a slug-like creature who lives on the planet Tatooine.

Prequel Playsets

Hasbro released playsets based on the prequel trilogy. One of the largest was Geonosis Battle Arena. This set hit shelves in 2002. Fans could re-create *Attack of the Clones* battles. The playset had two sides. One was a battle arena. The other was a droid factory. It also included Count Dooku's hangar.

One *Revenge of the Sith* playset featured Darth Sidious and Mace Windu on a battle platform. Kids could make the figures fight each other.

Hasbro released a BB-8 playset for younger kids. It was called the BB-8 Adventure Base.

The Last Jedi Playset

In 2017, Hasbro released another playset. It was the BB-8 Two-in-One Mega playset. This was part of The Last Jedi toy line. From outside, the playset looked like a large model of BB-8. He is a droid. The model opened. Inside was a multilevel playset. It included six settings. One was a Lightspeed Tracking Room. Another was a Detention Block.

Force Link Technology

The BB-8 playset had Force Link technology. Kids could wear a wristband. It activated lights and sounds on the playset. The set played phrases from the movie too.

Some *Force Awakens* sets came with multiple action figures and accessories. One set came with Rey, Finn, and the alien Maz Kanata.

VEHICLES

The original Star Wars films wowed audiences with their epic space battle scenes. The battle in *Return of the Jedi* features TIE Fighters, X-wings, and the *Millennium Falcon*.

Star Wars Ships

The Star Wars movies feature many amazing ships and other vehicles. Kenner created toy versions of many Star Wars vehicles. These could be used with action figures. The figures fit inside most vehicles.

The *TIE* in TIE Fighter is short for "twin ion engine." Kenner released several toy versions of this vehicle.

Flying through Space

Kenner included eight vehicles in its first Star Wars toy line. These came out between 1978 and 1979. Children could play with the Rebels' X-wing fighter ships. They could play with the Empire's TIE Fighters. There was a toy version of Darth Vader's TIE Fighter too.

Two action figures could fit in Kenner's 1978 Land Speeder. A 1979 version of the vehicle came with a remote control.

Land Speeder

Kenner released Luke Skywalker's Land Speeder in 1978. The toy had retractable wheels. The wheels were the same color as the speeder. This made it look as if the toy hovered over the ground.

Sandcrawler

Another toy was the Jawa Sandcrawler. It was released in 1979. In the movies, Jawas use this huge vehicle. It moves them across the desert. The toy came with a remote control. Kids used it to make the Sandcrawler move.

FUN FACT!

The Land Speeder's design was based on a small British car called the Bond Bug.

Jawas are small creatures with brown robes and glowing eyes. In *A New Hope*, they use the Sandcrawler to collect droids on Tatooine.

Millennium Falcon

Kenner released a toy *Millennium Falcon* in 1979. Kids could raise and lower the ship's ramp. The ship played battle alert sounds too.

Kenner's 1979 *Millennium Falcon* featured rotating guns, a radar dish, a smuggler's compartment, and a cockpit that opened and closed.

Many fans consider the *Millennium Falcon* to be the most iconic Star Wars spaceship. Many toys and models of the vehicle have been made.

Movie Details

Kenner's *Millennium Falcon* included many movie details. Action figures could sit at the ship's gaming table. They could sit in a gunner's chair. Luke Skywalker could practice using the Force with a training ball.

More Vehicles

The Empire Strikes Back introduced new Star Wars vehicles. Kenner made eight new vehicles based on the film. One was the Hoth Snowspeeder. Others were a Rebel Transport and an Imperial Cruiser.

FUN FACT!

The AT-AT is based on an extinct rhino-like species. It was the largest land animal to ever live.

AT-AT

Another toy was the Imperial All-Terrain Armored Transport (AT-AT). In the movies, this is one of

Kenner's Rebel Transport toy could hold 24 action figures. It featured a laser cannon and an escape hatch.

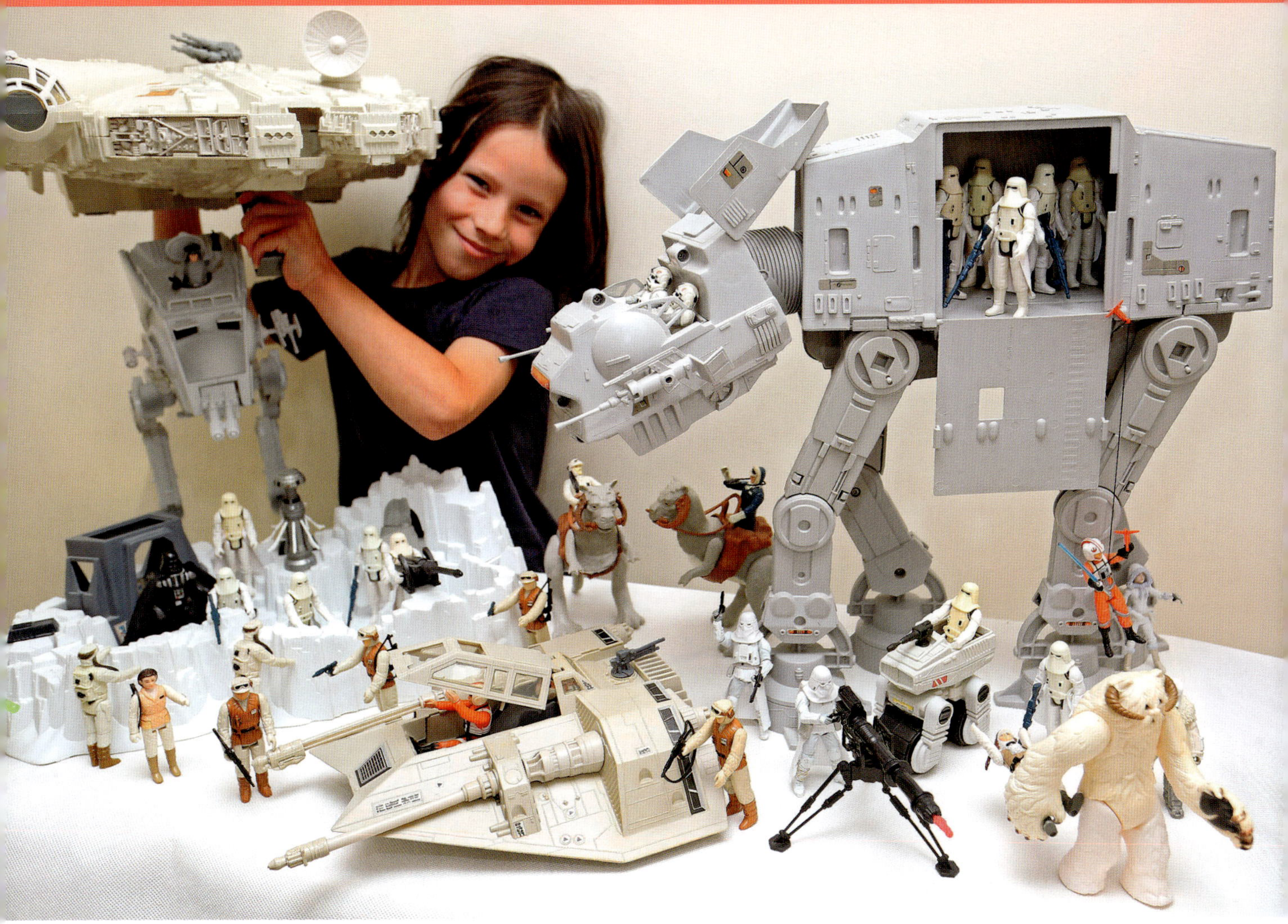

The Kenner AT-AT had missile launchers and laser cannons that lit up. Kids could open the vehicle's side door so action figures could ride inside it.

the Empire's vehicles. Action figures could ride in the AT-AT's cockpit. Kids could move the AT-AT's legs and feet. They could put it in battle position.

Mini-Rigs

For *The Empire Strikes Back*, Kenner created a new line of vehicles. They were called Mini-Rigs. These were smaller, cheaper toy vehicles. The CAP-2 and INT-4 were Mini-Rigs. They were released in 1982. Mini-Rigs sold well. Kenner released more in future toy lines.

One Mini-Rig was called the MTV-7. It came with a laser cannon and could hold one action figure.

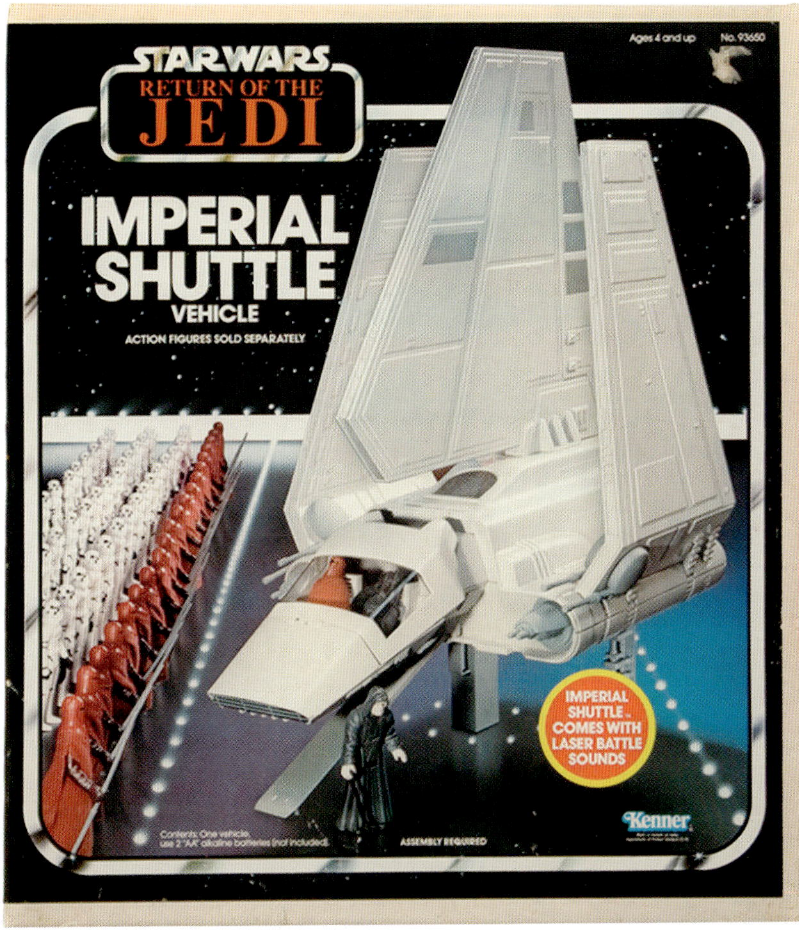

Kenner's 1984 Imperial Shuttle had adjustable pieces. Kids could push a button to change the position of the ship's wings.

Return of the Jedi Vehicles

Kenner released six new vehicles for *Return of the Jedi*. These included the B-Wing and Y-Wing. Other toys were the Speeder Bike, TIE Interceptor, and Imperial Shuttle. Kenner even sold a Battle-Damaged TIE Fighter.

Prequel and Sequel Vehicles

Hasbro released new vehicles based on the prequels. One was a small speeder. Another was the Naboo Royal Starship. Queen Padmé Amidala travels in this starship.

Hasbro's Phantom Menace toy line included vehicles such as podracers, droid fighters, and armored tanks.

Rey's Speeder

The sequel trilogy included new vehicles too. Toys of these came out between 2015 and 2016. One new vehicle was Rey's Speeder. It came with a Rey action figure.

Rey's Speeder came with a net and a missile launcher. Kids could press a button on the vehicle's side to shoot the missiles.

Role-Play Toys

Some Star Wars toys were role-play toys. These allowed fans to play like a Jedi. They could swing a lightsaber like Luke Skywalker. They could fire a blaster like Han Solo. They could even wear Darth Vader's mask.

FUN FACT!

Unlike a sword blade, a lightsaber's blade can cut in any direction.

A 1978 ad included pictures of Kenner's Star Wars Laser Pistol and Laser Rifle. Both toys made laser sounds.

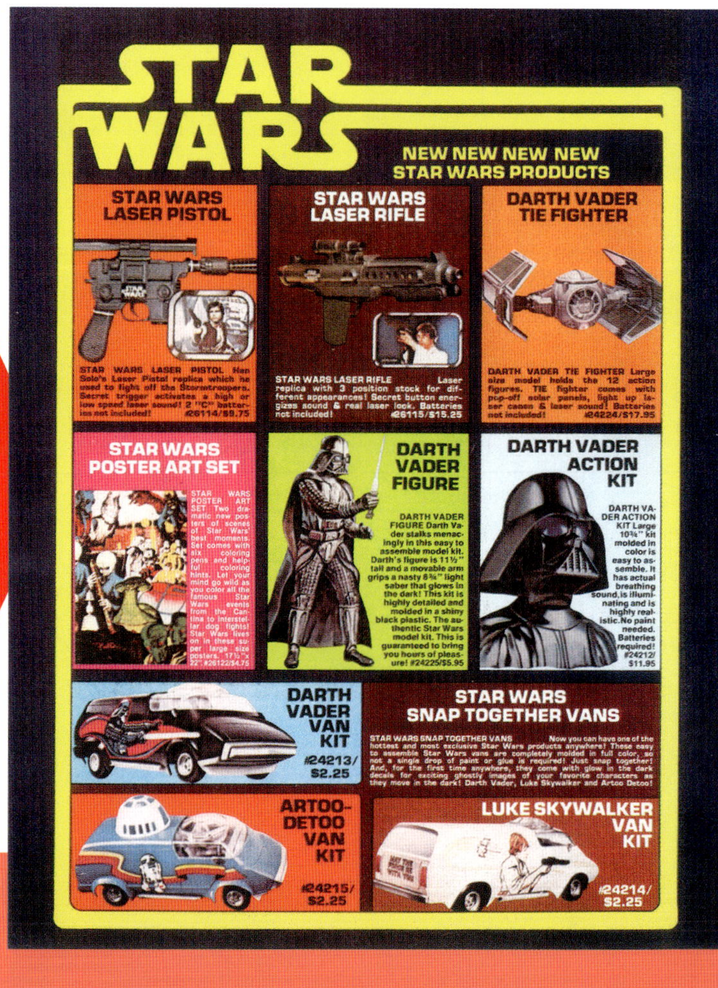

Original Lightsaber

Kenner released the first lightsaber toy in 1978. Designers attached a flashlight to an inflatable yellow blade. This toy often leaked air. Kenner included a repair kit in each package.

In *A New Hope*, Luke Skywalker uses a blue lightsaber that once belonged to his father, Anakin Skywalker.

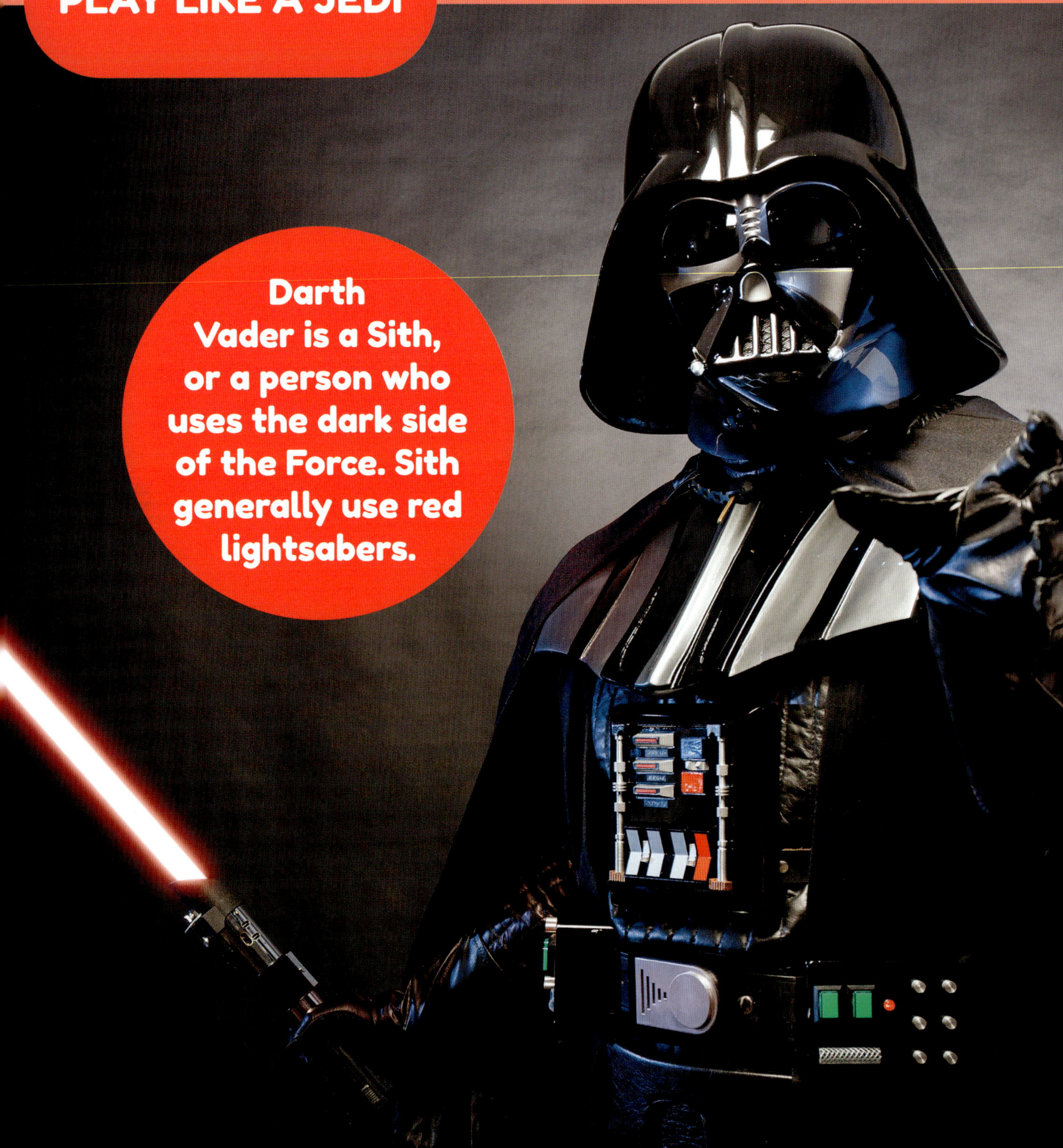

Darth Vader is a Sith, or a person who uses the dark side of the Force. Sith generally use red lightsabers.

Hasbro's 1996 electronic lightsabers could extend up to 3 feet (91 cm).

The Force Lightsaber

Kenner redesigned its lightsaber in 1980. The Force Lightsaber had a 3-foot (91 cm) hard plastic tube. It came in red or yellow.

Electronic Lightsabers

In 1996, Hasbro released two electronic lightsabers. Fans could choose Darth Vader's red lightsaber or Luke Skywalker's green one. The lightsabers had extendable blades. They lit up. They made sounds.

Fun Features

The Force Lightsaber had small holes at the blade's end. The holes made a whistling hum when the toy swung through the air.

Double Blade

Darth Maul is in *The Phantom Menace*. He is a Sith. He uses a double-bladed lightsaber. Hasbro released a toy version of it. It stretched 5 feet (1.5 m) from end to end. The electronic lightsaber had flashing lights. It made sounds.

FUN FACT!

In the Star Wars universe, lightsabers were first made by people on the dark side of the Force.

Build Your Own

In 2005, Hasbro let fans build their own lightsaber. It released a kit. The kit had more than 20 interchangeable parts. It featured electronic lights and sounds. Fans could put the parts together. They could make a custom lightsaber.

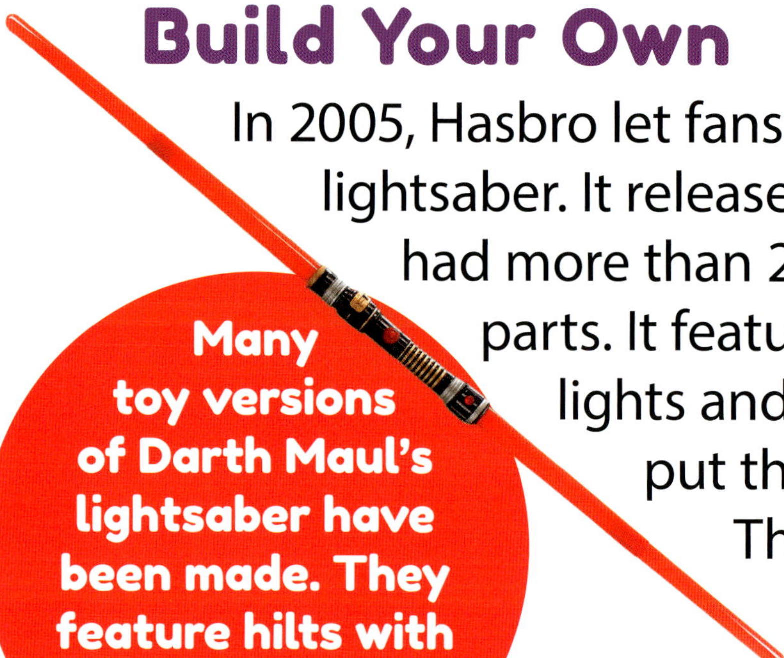

Many toy versions of Darth Maul's lightsaber have been made. They feature hilts with black-and-silver details.

Hasbro has made several versions of "build your own" lightsabers. Its Lightsaber Forge toy line included buildable lightsabers modeled after those of Star Wars characters.

The Ultimate FX Lightsaber made realistic "power up" and "power down" sounds. It also crackled and hummed when people hit it against another toy lightsaber.

Ultimate FX Lightsaber

The Ultimate FX Lightsaber came out in 2011. It lit up. It had motion-activated sounds. It came in several styles and colors. Some versions even had color-changing blades.

Bladebuilders

Bladebuilders were released in 2015. These took toy lightsabers to a new level. Kids could mix and match pieces. They could create all types of lightsabers. They could make double-sided blades. They could even make lightsabers with three blades.

Bladebuilders came with a variety of hilts and connector pieces so kids could customize their lightsabers. They could mix and match pieces from multiple Bladebuilder sets.

Hasbro's Force Awakens toy line included an electronic Chewbacca mask. It made roaring and growling sounds.

Helmets and Masks

Many Star Wars characters wear helmets and masks. Toy helmets and masks added new possibilities for play. Children could dress up as characters.

Darth Vader Mask

In the movies, Darth Vader wears a black mask and helmet. He has a deep voice. His suit also makes breathing noises. One toy mask included an electronic voice changer.

Hasbro's 2004 Darth Vader Voice Changer mask featured many sound effects, including recordings of Darth Vader's lines from the Star Wars films.

In the Star Wars films, Stormtroopers wear white armor. Many of them work on the Death Star.

Stormtrooper Mask

In Star Wars films, Stormtroopers wear white helmets. Masks with this design became popular toys. One had an electronic voice changer. The mask had a button. Kids pressed it to change their voices. It made them sound like a Stormtrooper.

Boba Fett Mask

A toy Boba Fett mask was also sold. Kids could dress up as the bounty hunter. They could press a button. This made sound effects play. The mask also played phrases from the films.

In the Star Wars films, Boba Fett's green helmet is scuffed and dented. Many toys and models of the helmet are designed to have the same markings.

Kenner's 1978 Laser Pistol toy had a secret button. When kids pressed the button, laser sounds played.

Other Weapons

Over the years, Kenner and Hasbro released Star Wars weapons besides lightsabers. One of the first was the 1978 Laser Pistol. Children could pretend to be Han Solo with this toy.

Water Guns and Foam Blasters

Hasbro produced several Star Wars water guns. They also made foam blasters. One was the Nerf

Super Soaker Chewbacca Bowcaster. This toy looks like the character's iconic weapon. It can shoot water up to 38 feet (11.6 m).

Star Wars Guns

In the Star Wars movies, blasters and pistols fire bolts of intense energy.

The Nerf Super Soaker Chewbacca Bowcaster was part of The Force Awakens toy line. It featured orange and gray colors.

Star Wars Games

Kenner released two Star Wars board games in 1977. One was called Star Wars: Escape from Death Star. Players roll dice or use a spinner. This tells them how to move around the board. Players complete missions. They try to escape. They must get to the *Millennium Falcon*. The first player to reach the Rebel Base wins.

Star Wars: Escape from Death Star came with a dotted game board and an R2-D2 spinner. The game tokens featured images of Han Solo, Princess Leia, Luke, and Chewbacca.

Star Wars: Destroy Death Star was based on the space battle in *A New Hope*. During the battle, Luke pilots an X-wing and shoots the Death Star's exhaust port.

Back-to-Back Play

Star Wars: Destroy Death Star continues the story. Each player has three X-wings. They move around a Death Star game board. To win, players must land on the Death Star exhaust port. In the movie, this is the Death Star's weak point.

Special Editions

Since 1977, many Star Wars board games have been created. Some are classic board games with a Star Wars theme. Fans can play Star Wars Monopoly. There are also Star Wars editions of Uno and Battleship. Fans can even play Star Wars Trivial Pursuit.

Star Wars Monopoly includes game pieces shaped like popular characters. In the game, players buy and sell Star Wars vehicles.

Clue: Star Wars

Clue is another popular board game. Players solve a murder mystery. There is a Star Wars version of the game. People play as Star Wars characters. They move around the board. They try to find out Darth Vader's next target.

Clue: Star Wars comes with a 3D game board shaped like the Death Star. It also includes six character game pieces.

Strategy Games

Many Star Wars board games are strategy games. In these, winners and losers are not decided by luck. Instead, each player makes decisions. These affect what happens in the game. Star Wars: Rebellion is a popular strategy game. Players command starships. They plan troop movements and gather allies. The game comes with more than 150 plastic pieces. These include characters and vehicles.

There are several Star Wars versions of popular strategy games such as chess. One Star Wars chess set comes with silver character game pieces.

In 2007, the Star Wars Pocketmodel TCG trading card game came out. It featured trading cards and miniature models of ships and vehicles.

Trading Card Games

Trading card games involve strategy. But they also involve collecting cards. One example is Star Wars: Destiny. It is a collectible card and dice game. It was released in 2016. Players use dice and cards to battle each other.

Play at Home

In 1982, Parker Brothers released the first Star Wars video game. It was called *Star Wars: The Empire Strikes Back*. It was made for the Atari 2600 gaming system. Players battle on Hoth. They defend a Rebel base from the Empire.

In the 1982 *Empire Strikes Back* game, players pilot a Snowspeeder and try to shoot AT-AT walkers.

Star Wars Outlaws **came out in 2024. In this open-world video game, players explore the galaxy as the outlaw Kay Vess.**

World of Games

Since 1982, more than 100 Star Wars video games have been released. Some are first-person shooter games. Others are strategy games. There are also racing and action-adventure games.

Gamers could try playing an updated version of *Star Wars: Battlefront* at the Paris Games Week event in 2015.

Star Wars: Battlefront

Star Wars: Battlefront is a popular series. The first game was released in 2004. Battlefront games are shooter games. Gamers play as soldiers. They fight in different Star Wars armies.

Lego Star Wars: The Video Game

Lego Star Wars: The Video Game came out in 2005. It is a Lego-themed action-adventure game. It is the first in a series of Lego Star Wars video games. It was designed for children.

Many Lego Star Wars video games have been released. The 2022 game *Lego Star Wars: The Skywalker Saga* features characters and stories from all nine films.

In 2011, the video game *Star Wars: The Old Republic* came out. Creators discussed updates to the game at a 2012 conference.

Star Wars: The Force Unleashed

Star Wars: The Force Unleashed was released in 2008. In this game, people play as Starkiller. He is Darth Vader's apprentice. Starkiller has been trained to hunt Jedi. The game is an origin story. It shows how the Galactic Civil War started.

Star Wars Jedi: Fallen Order

In 2019, *Star Wars Jedi: Fallen Order* came out. This game is set five years after *Revenge of the Sith*. Gamers play as Cal Kestis. He is one of the last Jedi. Kestis must complete his Jedi training. He must restore the Jedi Order.

In *Star Wars Jedi: Fallen Order*, players explore the galaxy, battle villains, and learn new lightsaber skills.

Lego Sets

In 1999, Lego released its first Star Wars products. These included construction sets and minifigures. Since then, there have been more than 700 Star Wars Lego sets. More than 1,000 minifigures have been released. Lego Star Wars sets feature popular characters. They also feature Star Wars settings and vehicles.

Many Star Wars Lego sets feature iconic vehicles from the films, such as TIE Fighters, speeder bikes, and Boba Fett's starship.

Death Star

The Lego Death Star includes 4,016 pieces. It is a multilevel set. It includes a trash compactor. It also has a droid maintenance room. Fans can re-create movie scenes with the set. It comes with 23 minifigures.

Lucasfilm and Lego

Lucasfilm is a production company. George Lucas started it. It makes movies and TV shows. In 1998, the Lego company signed a Star Wars licensing agreement with Lucasfilm. It was Lego's first step into movie licensing.

The Lego Death Star includes many details from *A New Hope*. These include a trash compactor with moving walls and a swiveling planet destroyer with lasers.

The Lego AT-AT comes with spring-loaded missile shooters and a side panel that opens. Lego minifigures can sit inside the AT-AT's cockpit.

AT-AT

One Lego set features an AT-AT. Builders create the vehicle out of 1,267 pieces. They can pose the AT-AT's limbs. The set comes with several minifigures. One is Luke Skywalker.

Battle of Endor

Another Lego set is The Battle of Endor. It re-creates the battle from *Return of the Jedi*. The set features a bunker with sliding doors. It also includes a firing catapult. It comes with two speeder bikes and 12 minifigures.

FUN FACT!

In 2013, Lego unveiled a life-size model of an X-wing starfighter. The huge sculpture was made out of 5.3 million Lego bricks.

The Lego Battle of Endor set has 890 pieces and includes Han Solo, Princess Leia, and Ewok minifigures.

Podracers

One Lego set features two podracers. These are racing vehicles. They are featured in the prequels. The set includes 810 pieces. Builders can re-create the race between Anakin Skywalker and Sebulba. The set includes five minifigures.

In the Lego podracer set, Sebulba's podracer is orange and gray. Anakin Skywalker's podracer is gray, blue, and yellow.

The Lego Republic Gunship was released in 2013. It includes missile launchers, gun turrets, and multiple doors.

Republic Gunship

The Lego Republic Gunship includes 1,175 pieces. It has large doors that swing open. Minifigures can ride inside. The gunship comes with several minifigures. One is Obi-Wan Kenobi. Others include Anakin Skywalker and Padmé Amidala.

Duel on Mustafar

One Lego set features the Duel on Mustafar. This is a battle between Anakin Skywalker and Obi-Wan Kenobi. It happens in *Revenge of the Sith*. The set includes 208 pieces. It has two sliding platforms.

Many *Revenge of the Sith* Lego sets include Anakin Skywalker minifigures with long brown hair and black robes.

In the Star Wars sequels, Poe Dameron's X-wing is orange and black. The Lego version of the ship has wings that can open and close.

Poe's X-Wing Fighter

Poe's X-Wing Fighter is a 717-piece Lego set. It is based on Poe Dameron's X-wing. Poe is a character in the sequel trilogy. The ship's wings open. Its landing gear retracts. The ship's cockpit opens. It can hold minifigures.

The Snoke's Throne Room Lego set includes a rotating throne with a hidden compartment underneath it. It comes with weapons such as lightsabers and staffs.

Snoke's Throne Room

Snoke's Throne Room is a 492-piece Lego set. It features Supreme Leader Snoke's rotating throne room. This setting appears in the sequels. The Lego set has a turning doorway and moving floors. It also has compartments. These hold treasures and weapons. The set comes with five minifigures. These include Rey, Kylo Ren, and Snoke.

Millennium Falcon

The first Lego *Millennium Falcon* was released in 2000. There have been 12 Lego versions of the ship. One version came out in 2017. It has 7,541 pieces. It is the largest Star Wars Lego set ever made.

The 2017 Lego *Millennium Falcon* comes with minifigures from both the sequels and the original trilogy. The set sells for hundreds of dollars.

The Mandalorian

The Mandalorian is a live-action television series. It first aired in 2019. The series introduces a new character, Grogu. He is a young Jedi. He looks like a baby Yoda. The popular series has inspired many toys. There are action figures and masks. There are also lightsabers and plush toys.

FUN FACT!

In *Revenge of the Sith,* Anakin Skywalker kills many young Jedi in the Jedi temple. Grogu survives the attack.

In *The Mandalorian,* Grogu is often called "the Child." Action figures and plush toys of this character are popular with fans.

One Mandalorian Lego set is called Trouble on Tatooine. It includes a speeder bike and a Tusken Raider hut.

Universe of Toys

Kids can enjoy many Mandalorian toys and games. They can build Mandalorian Lego sets. They can play board games. One is Monopoly: Star Wars: The Mandalorian Edition.

Vintage Collection

The Mandalorian led to the creation of the Vintage Collection. This toy line features modern figures inspired by the original Kenner action figures.

GLOSSARY

acetate
A material made from wood pulp combined with chemicals.

bounty hunter
Someone who is paid to track people down and capture them.

collectible
Describing an item that is valued or wanted for a collection.

custom
Specially made for a specific person or purpose.

droid
A robot that acts and sometimes looks like a human.

franchise
A brand or business.

imperial
Having to do with an empire.

interchangeable
Able to be switched and used in place of something else, such as a part.

mold
A hollow container used to make a consistent shape.

prequel
An installment in a book or movie series that takes place in the past, before an installment released earlier.

retract
To pull back in or collapse.

sculpt
To carve or mold into a specific shape or object.

sequel
An installment in a book or movie series that takes place in the future, after an installment released earlier.

silicone
A flexible, rubber-like material.

trilogy
A series of three related works.

vinyl
A type of tough, shiny plastic.

TO LEARN MORE

More Books to Read

Abdo, Kenny. *Star Wars Franchise*. Abdo, 2025.

Beecroft, Simon, and Pablo Hidalgo. *Star Wars Character Encyclopedia Updated and Expanded Edition*. DK, 2021.

Dowsett, Elizabeth. *LEGO Star Wars Character Encyclopedia*. DK, 2020.

Online Resources

Booklinks
NONFICTION NETWORK
FREE! ONLINE NONFICTION RESOURCES

To learn more about Star Wars, please visit **abdobooklinks.com** or scan this QR code. These links are routinely monitored and updated to provide the most current information available.

INDEX

PHOTO CREDITS

Cover Photos: Adobe Stock, front (Grogu, green light saber, red light saber), back; Willrow Hood/Shutterstock Images, front (figures); BrendanHunter/iStock Unreleased/Getty Images, front (Millennium Falcon)

Interior Photos: Iridiumphotographics/iStock Unreleased/Getty Images, 1; Turac Novruzova/Shutterstock Images, 3, 45 (top), 55 (bottom); LMPC/Getty Images, 4; George Widman/AP Images, 5; Sunset Boulevard/Corbis Historical/Getty Images, 6, 14, 44, 89; Arthur Sidey/Mirrorpix/Getty Images, 7, 80; iStockphoto, 8, 18, 35, 37, 38, 59 (top), 61, 73, 75; Vsevolod Udanov/Shutterstock Images, 9 (top); Aaron Lim/Shutterstock Images, 9 (bottom); Frazer Harrison/Getty Images Entertainment/Getty Images, 10; Shutterstock Images, 11 (light sabers, helmets, Millennium Falcon, gun, AT-AT, TIE fighter, BB-8, X-wing), 13 (bottom), 25 (right), 32 (left), 57, 59 (bottom), 63 (top), 65, 91 (bottom), 92, 93, 101 (top), 113, 115 (top), 115 (bottom), 124, 125 (top), 125 (bottom); Vadim Sazhniev/Shutterstock Images, 11 (Death Star, R2-D2); Amy Sussman/Getty Images Entertainment/Getty Images, 12; Artur Widak/NurPhoto/Getty Images, 13 (top); Steve Mack/S. D. Mack Pictures/Alamy, 15; Don Emmert/AFP/Getty Images, 16; www.benstoybarn.com/Alamy, 17, 21, 22, 27, 28, 33, 45 (bottom), 48, 68, 82, 85; Oli Scarff/AFP/Getty Images, 19; Chris Willson/Alamy, 20, 25 (left), 26, 29, 32 (right); Insidefoto srl/Alamy Live News/Insidefoto di Andrea Staccioli/Alamy, 23; Willrow Hood/Shutterstock Images, 24, 30, 39, 41, 43, 55 (top), 56, 58, 79, 103; Aaron Roe/Alamy, 31; Lucasfilm/Sunset Boulevard/Corbis Historical/Getty Images, 34, 36, 67, 70; Soeren Schulz/Alamy, 40, 42, 84; Christian Liliendahl/Gonzales Photo/Alamy, 46; Matthew Corrigan/Shutterstock Images, 47; Andrew Matthews/PA Images/Getty Images, 49; Su Hsun/Shutterstock Images, 50; powerofforever/iStock Unreleased/Getty Images, 51; Evan Agostini/Hulton Archive/Getty Images, 52, 53; George Best/Getty Images Entertainment/Getty Images, 54; Lucas Films/Bad Robot/Walt Disney Productions/Album/Alamy, 60; Tibrina Hobson/Getty Images Entertainment/Getty Images, 62, 87; Jeff Bukowski/Shutterstock Images, 63 (bottom); Globalimages101/Alamy, 64; Peter Williams/PRWPhotography/Alamy, 66, 78, 83; Whitney Hayward/Portland Press Herald/Getty Images, 69; Izwan Is/Shutterstock Images 71; Ryan Gale/Red Line Editorial, 72; Charles Sykes/Invision for Hasbro/AP Images, 74; Screen Archives/Moviepix/Getty Images, 76, 98; BrendanHunter/iStock Unreleased/Getty Images, 77, 81, 106; Jonathan Elderfield/Hulton Archive/Getty Images, 86; adsR/Alamy, 88; Stefano Buttafoco/Shutterstock Images, 90; Courtesy of The Strong National Museum of Play, Rochester, New York, USA, 91 (top), 100, 105; Jason Kempin/Getty Images Entertainment/Getty Images, 94; Ki Price/Corbis News/Getty Images, 95; David Cardinez/Shutterstock Images, 96; Business Wire/Getty Images Publicity/Getty Images, 97; Barry Brecheisen/WireImage/Getty Images, 99; Nerf Wiki, 101 (bottom); Susie Kearley/Alamy, 102; Sean Dempsey/PA Images/Getty Images, 104; Michael Tullberg/Getty Images Entertainment/Getty Images, 107; ArcadeImages/Alamy, 108; Chesnot/Getty Images Entertainment/Getty Images, 109; Chesnot/Getty Images News/Getty Images, 110; Miguel Lagoa/Shutterstock Images, 111; Joe Klamar/AFP/Getty Images, 112; Justin Sullivan/Getty Images News/Getty Images, 114; Puha Dorin/Shutterstock Images, 116; Burcu Ergin/Shutterstock Images, 117, 118, 121; Levent Konuk/Shutterstock Images, 119, 120; Andrey Arkusha/Shutterstock Images, 122; Jakub Porzycki/Anadolu Agency/Getty Images, 123